viva loss

sarah fran wisby

D1484435

small desk press **san francisco**

Published by Small Desk Press
PO Box 170232
San Francisco, California 94117-0232
www.smalldeskpress.com

ISBN-10: 0-9789858-2-6
ISBN-13: 978-0-9789858-2-0

for the losers, and for the light

ACKNOWLEDGMENTS

Very special thanks to Toni Mirosevich, Nona Caspers, and Michelle Carter for years of inspiration and encouragement, to my parents (all of you) for a lifetime of support, to Kim Pierce and Philip Dachelet for the dog-sitting and so much more, to Rainbow Grocery Cooperative for the camaraderie and sustenance, and to all my teachers, whether loving or harsh, for instructing me in the ways of the world.

ring out the bells that still can ring
forget your perfect offering
there is a crack in everything
that's how the light gets in

—Leonard Cohen

I

HIGH DRAMA

What if you were dying, and I came to you with my hair down, my mouth soft, my axis stilled, and you knew there wasn't time to find anyone better, who shared your taste in movies and alcohol, who wasn't crazy, who knew the right things to say to make you love her, and you were in a fever, and I was your nurse, and utterly selfless, and you were scared, but not in a way that closed you off, but paradoxically lifted you to a higher plane, where fear was a holy thing, and you wanted to share it with someone, and I was scared too, but with a glistening edge like a planet coming out of shadow.

What if I was dying, and you came to visit me, and my hair was arranged just so on the pillow, and the heat was rising from my body, and you were caught up in the swirling tragedy of the moment, and you knew it wouldn't be much longer, and that later you could say you had loved a girl who was now dead, and that would give you a sort of street cred

in the dating world, a mystique that women would find irresistible. What if I resisted you, if in dying I achieved the sort of pride that evaded me in life, what if I told you to go to hell, and take your nursing skills elsewhere, and leave me to die in peace, and what if you didn't leave, and instead peeled the sheet gently back from my body, and picked up a sponge and started washing me with it, drenching the fiery hollows, murmuring to me in a low, strange voice you didn't understand, had never heard before, didn't know you were capable of.

1. I'm ready for my Brompton cocktail. The light on my face, the melting arias. Given the right chemicals all devils turn angel. Come to me, Doctor, and make me well. Maketh me to lie down, my limbs aligned and my fluttering stilled.

The stars are worse off. They've got to shine and shine and shine. I've got pills and sleep and hope. They're all alone, the darkness pecking at them from all sides. I've got electric lights, umbrellas, a teakettle, a CD player, an Electrolux vacuum cleaner from the fifties.

Never underestimate the power of contraptions.

2. Nature is untouchably lovely, yet we've touched her all over, mined her for metaphors, fucked her various clefts. She holds us by the corners, like something soiled.

133. EXHILARATING AGENCY OF LIGHT
from the book of light

I spend my days looking at boys, my nights in semi-grateful reverie for the way light plays in their hair and flicks the creases of their jeans. How light coats each eyelash and floods each milk-boat eye. But if I were honest I would say I hate the light, for all the surfaces it gets to touch while I stand on the bank of its endlessness, hands jammed in my pockets, looking. My eye can crawl all over him without leaving a scratch. It is only when our eyes meet, and we are brave or wanton enough to withstand the gaze—a kind of light itself—that eyes become more than empty dinner plates for pictures of food to flit across.

134. ANCIENT CONCEPTIONS OF LIGHT
from the book of light

The ancients believed that some boys were made of light, and had strong ropes woven out of selkie-hair and queenslashes with which to bind them to pillars in the great hall, so that all could gather in ceremony to sup on the light. But the boys kept burning through the ropes and running away together, spitting into their palms and shaking hands as if to seal some oath of loyalty. They hopped freight trains and slept, rose resplendent, and dove from open, glowing boxcars into swimming holes deep in the forest where only they could see. Though they could not hide, for their light trailed after them like foggy phosphorus tails, nor could they be caught, for light was always one step ahead of sound. In the time it took for one of us to give the cry, "Yonder boylight!" our boys were long gone. Only a shimmer remained, and that just a ghost on the retina, though it appeared to rustle the trees.

135. NEWTON'S VIEW OF ITS NATURE
from the book of light

Nowadays, of course, we know that boys are not themselves constructed of light. It was only the lens of longing, coupled with a savage ignorance, that confused the ancients and caused them to mistake such boys for the truly luminous bodies—the Sun, the Moon, the Television—the pleats of whose gowns settle democratically over us all.

Sir Isaac Newton hypothesized that certain boys were hollow, like funnels, or like the chambers of seashells, and that was why they so effortlessly collected and refracted the light while the rest of us nibbled bitterly at our rationed rays. Sir Isaac built elaborate traps with mirrored chutes and light-tight boxes, but he couldn't figure out what to use as bait. They didn't seem to want anything, our bright hollow boys. At last he settled on a plan of burning various hardwood logs, cherry and hickory, the scent of which was said to be agreeable to them.

I used to creep to the edge of his property and watch him tending the fires in a huge black grate. His normally round and jovial face appeared gauntly demonic from the harsh underlighting, and his sweat dripped and sizzled in the coals.

Sometimes, high above our town, the cloudy night sky lit up unevenly with boylight. Pale lavender flashes, then bright ones of a silvery green, leapt from cloud to cloud. On those nights the whole town joined in Newton's wonder, forgave his madness, threw back our heads to ogle the sky, though in the morning our stiff necks and aching jaws issued swift admonition. But Newton would not be placated by a light show. "Show yourselves!" he thundered. And then, trembling, "please."

On one such night he proved the dangers of boy-obsession by throwing himself atop his own bonfire. When we reached him he was a blackened husk, but before that, as we raced toward the flames, we heard him cry out, "At last, at last!" for in burning, he took the flames for bright boys licking him all over his person.

136. LIGHT GAINS INTENSITY AS IT IS APPROACHED

from the book of light

I have discovered, through a series of shoddily unscientific experiments—none of which would stand up to reasoned scrutiny by a qualified professional, but which are nonetheless extremely valuable to me—that the type of light manifested in boys, while it can be trained, prefers to play. It likes to splay out undisturbed in a darkened room and see how far its tentacles will unfurl. It likes to listen to raunchy unrelenting rock and roll music, and feel its own crackling edges disintegrate. It will let you get quite close to it. It will even let you stroke its excited particles which stutter and fizzle out and come back to life in an ever-renewing fountain of light, provided you do not allow your greed to overtake you and lunge at the base of the fountain, the stony body of the boy in question. The boy may submit to such rough, bossy handling, but the light will not, and the light, after all, is what you are after.

137. HOW BODIES RECEIVE THE LUMINOUS PRINCIPLE
from the book of light

In truth, the light recoils from his body, and plunges away from it in all directions. This is what makes him seem to shine. My dark eye drinks him thus, drinks and drinks the light that cannot find a pathway to his dark places. Sometimes I think all this light-guzzling will lead me to find what the light cannot, the chink in the armor, the tiniest pinhole. But the light doesn't care about any of this. The light just lands where it lands. His eyelids, my breasts, his earlobes, my ankles. A sort of web builds up between us through every spot we touch. Threads of light like the softest of fur. It's hard to stop. I cover his body with my body, try to harness the light. But he thrashes this way and that and I'm losing him, the drops of light fly everywhere from his skin. They hang in the air like a thousand mocking stars, and I still can't look away.

VIVA LOSS

A photograph is a dead skin you shimmy out of. This one's still alive, white virus blooming at its center. The flash nearly blots out its subject: a man and a woman in a hotel bathroom mirror, cheap metal sconces on either side, low ceiling pressing down like a thundercloud. The woman cradles the camera, steadying it against her abdomen, her hands white gloves where they disappear into light. Her hair is vaporous, coal-black. Her grey fox coat hangs open, the fur damp-looking and shiny. She wears nothing underneath but a black bra, its ribbon a clear pink, like a cat's tongue.

The man in the photo is blurred. Moving toward her or away, it's impossible to tell. He's naked to the waist, the flesh of his exposed chest like something prised from a shell. He embraces the woman, bending around her, his arms in surprisingly sharp focus, right down to the gold hair on his forearms, the gold ring on his left hand. One

arm rests casually around her shoulders, the other reaches inside the coat for her waist. He touches the fur and the flesh underneath. If we could read his mind it would say *my, my, my, my, my.* Not in a proprietary sense. Appreciative. Purr of a well-oiled engine.

He's got money in his pocket, a plane to catch. She's got a bottle to polish off, curtains to yank free from their rods and wrap around her body. What is pleasure if it leads us here? The photo holds no answer. That's why I can't put it down. The man's eye in the mirror is heavy-lidded, half-closed, half-dispensing its murky light. Picture an aquarium, lit by electric eels. Behind them, endless beige tile. Outside the frame: the desert lapping at the edge of town, dark sea around this bright island. Also: the cold night dissolving its stars, the lights of the strip cheapening the dawn, the future plotting even lovelier mistakes, my own among them. The woman's eyes are neither here nor there. Somewhere between the ceiling and the sky. Call it the middle distance. If we could read her. If we could read her.

II

THE PLECOSTOMUS AND THE ANGELFISH

We lay flat in cool grass. Above the tops of the trees shapes were turning, the vast shark-like bodies of bomber jets prowling the sky. They reminded me of something, so at last I had a story to tell: My parents had a fish tank, and one night they came home to find the plecostomus sucking the angelfish. A week later the angelfish was dead, and the plecostomus went back to his job of cleaning the slime from the walls of the tank. What the hell kind of a story is that, my friends cried, when we are lying here terrified of bombs. It's a true story, I replied.

VERTIGO

A young woman walks into the cafe with a grown-up hairdo. Butterscotch blonde, combed and twisted and coiled around itself with no ends showing, like a snake eating its own tail. At the back of her head, near the spot which in infancy was soft before the plates of the skull grew to cover it, the hairdo forms a vortex like the nest of a fastidious bird, or like the beckoning frothy tunnel an electric mixer drills in a bowl of cream. It is a hairdo copied from an old movie, worn by a woman with something to hide. I picture the original mastermind behind this hairdo, holding a rat-tailed comb, his own hair neatly trimmed the way his mother used to do it. *You will be as a rabbit-hole,* he tells the woman whose hair lies parted and ready, an unreaped field, *for unwitting men to tumble down.*

Once upon a time the son of a basket-maker was condemned to death by a tyrant queen. His mother bribed the executioner to let her weave the basket that would catch her son's head. She wove a spell into the straw that would keep his head alive for three days and three nights. The axe fell and the head dropped and the distraught woman carried it away. But the spell worked, and for three days and three nights she lay in bed with her son's head, caressing its pale brow. She spoke to it, telling such stories as she had told him as a boy, of naughty rabbits who stole from the farmer's cabbage rows, and goose girls who lay down in the field with shepherds. *Your stories, mother,* the young man mouthed, for his larynx was below the chopmark, *made me think there was no such thing as sin.*

Forgive me, the old woman said. *Our lessons were cut short. I would have taught you everything I know: how to sin, and how to escape the notice of the queen.*

THREE DEVILS

Henry hadn't been drunk for several years, and even then he was never a hallucinating drunk. He would simply sit at the kitchen table all night and pour one shot after the next until he saw nothing, heard nothing, became a snoring heap for his children to maneuver around in the morning as they made their sandwiches for school. The only time he was really an inconvenience was when he'd shit his pants, and his eldest, Sonia, had to roll him onto the floor and, with the help of her brother Jacob, wrestle the pants from his two hundred pound frame and clean him up with paper towels and liquid soap. This would sometimes make them late for school, and Sonia, a fastidious girl, worried that she had not been able to entirely remove the stink from her hands, sniffed at them constantly, and washed between every class. But really this hadn't happened very often, and his children had forgiven him, had even come to his graduation from rehab, Sonia in a black dress printed with

small blue trumpet flowers and Jacob in his beat-up brown leather jacket.

So, when he saw the devils cavorting in his kitchen sink drain, lithe and slippery and red as Vienna sausages, laughing up at his astonished face from the just-scoured chrome, he wondered what they wanted with him. The first devil climbed onto the metal knob of the drain stopper. "Your daughter will never marry," he chortled. He had a face like a soiled rag and a forked tail covered in scabs. "She is unable to love." He took a little bow, and the other two devils burst out laughing, then knocked him off his perch and sparred for who would go next. The winner leapt onto the knob and balanced on one rotten foot, spreading a pair of veiny, blotched wings. "Your son is a drug addict." This proclamation brought clapping and hoots from the other two. "He shoots the heroin in between his fingers and toes so that no one will see the marks. He hires prostitutes to shoot him up, he cannot perform sexually, his girlfriend thinks it's her fault and makes herself throw up." He then pantomimed shoving his fingers down his throat and retching over and over to the delight of his companions.

Henry clutched the edge of the countertop, trembling. He kept one eye on the chopping knife in the silverware drain he would use to chop them into writhing bits before rinsing them into the jaws of the garbage disposal, yet was unable to move until he'd heard the rest of their message. The third devil removed his top hat and held it to his chest with feigned solemnity, circled the drain and stepped up to the stopper. He wore a waistcoat made from blood-encrusted feathers, beneath it his penis swung like a club. "You will live to be a very old man," he intoned. "You will marry twice more, and retire early with plenty of money. You will never have another drink, and will never stop wanting one. You will watch your children conceal their suffering for your sake, and you will be grateful for this, though something will nag at you inside. You will forget all about us in a few moments, as soon as we are gone. We will be the sad kernels of your heart speaking a language you don't understand." And with that, the three devils slithered silently down the drain, and Henry, his hand reaching half-heartedly now for the knife, did not know what he wanted it for.

BOYS CARRIED HER OUT INTO THE FIELD

They were little boys, first graders from her brother's class. She had come around from the big kids' side of school to collect him so they could walk home together, as they sometimes did. Maybe she felt lonely; maybe a friend had betrayed her to walk home with someone else. Her brother was gone from the playground, everyone was gone except for some rough-looking boys who came toward her across the sandbox, kicking up dust. She thought she might as well ask them if they'd seen her brother, and the one boy snickered as if it were a dirty sort of question. Then he gave a signal or maybe he just said *Get Her* and the boys grabbed her arms and legs and carried her out into the field. She struggled and kicked and twisted back and forth. It was the oddest sort of feeling, like floating, all of her effort simply absorbed by whatever substance held her afloat. The boys laid her down in the grass and sat on her arms and legs. She was like Gulliver, captured by Lilliputians. The cen-

terfold drawing in her <u>Gulliver's Travels</u> picture book showed him bound by ropes to the ground; his enormous size compared to his captors' tiny bodies was somehow obscene. The leader of the boys came and lay down on top of her. The hair on the top of his head was thick and rust-colored, and when he glanced at her face she saw sallow, freckled skin, a curled lip. He made quick cursory movements with his hands, passing them over her breasts. Her held breath burned her lungs. He was so young to be so bad. She knew what it was like to be bad—she had been bad for a long, long time. She'd stolen money from her mother's purse. She'd told lies, read a filthy book from her father's bookshelf, smoked a cigarette. She'd written a letter to a boy she liked, telling him all the things she'd like to do to him, with words she found in the filthy book, then signed her best friend's name to it. The rusty-haired boy rubbed his hands—they were so small—between her legs, over the bumpy zipper of her jeans, and a burning feeling crept over her, humiliation and something else. Then all the boys sprang up at once as if from some subtle signal or a shared knowledge that their work was done. They ran away laughing and she could finally move, though now there was no reason to.

THE PORTABLE GRAVE

He carries it with him, everywhere he goes. Someone told him he would have eternal nightmares if he died and wasn't buried in hallowed ground. So he went to the churchyard and dug up some earth and filled a pouch and sewed it inside his shirt just above his solar plexus. That way if he died he would lie under hallowed ground no matter if anyone bothered to bury him. These were plague times and many were left unburied, dumped in huge piles on the outskirts of town.

But what if I fall forward?

He made another pouch and filled it with more dirt, sewed it into the back of his shirt, and congratulated himself on his readiness. Everywhere he went he could smell the loamy scent rising from his chest and he felt safe and loved. His village was a mess. The stench of death was everywhere. As if that wasn't bad enough, people who were other-

wise healthy were hell-bent on killing themselves through drink or killing their neighbors for the smallest slights. He was lucky to love God and to love himself. The odors that rose from his body, not just the dirt but the sweat and the semen and the stench of his faraway feet—all the smells of a man—reminded him of that.

But what if I fall to one side?

He liked to sleep on his side with his legs tucked up next to him, so it made sense that he might die in this position, too. He made two more pouches and fastened them to his belt loops, one on either side. They swung there and he felt their weight like a second pair of testicles, only these were designed to protect him and not the other way around. Some people carried posies, to ward off disease. He did not believe in tampering with God's will. The soul is a flower and it will open only after God has plucked it.

What if I stumble and fall into a cistern, head first with my legs in the air like branches?

Ha! He knew he was getting carried away, but the

more he thought about this possibility, the more it troubled him. He pictured the tree of his wronged body, first with his pants hanging off in tatters, then his flesh, and then with noisy birds nesting in his bones. How would he ever rest? It would be like trying to sleep with no eyelids under a bright sun. He crept back to the churchyard with his trowel and ten tiny sacks. He would tie one to each of his toes and be done with it. He would lay down his horror of death and go on with the business of living. He would take a wife and store his life in her body. He would give her everything he had, which was nothing, but it would become something inside of her. The spot he had chosen to gather his dirt was atop a freshly dug grave, where the soil was looser and he could just scoop it into the bags. Suddenly a voice called to him to stop. A light shone in his face.

The penalty for grave robbing was death by hanging, even if all you stole was dirt. They hung him in the forest from a low branch because they were in a hurry. His toes dangled inches from the ground so that it was easy to mistake him from a distance for a man walking toward you at an incredibly slow pace. Children shouted at him and threw

sticks, and when he did not move they came closer and dared one another to poke at him. The man who was supposed to cut him down either forgot or died of plague. His tongue swelled up purple and eventually burst, staining his shirt. Birds came to nest in his skeleton.

And what if I die upright, standing at the ready, waiting for God to pluck me?

III

A PROPOSITION

I'm a mumbler, you're a mumbler. Let's have a conversation where we have to lean closer and closer to hear what the other is saying until our ears are crushed up against each other's busy lips fumbling numb language.

THE PEOPLE MOVER

Step on, step on. Feel the soft give of rubber padding under woven steel. Try to relax. You could be inert yet carried. Incomprehensible, yet conveyed. You grab the rail, or does the rail grab you? You could hold it all the way, gently tugging at your hand like a benign child. Let it go. Surge forward with the current. Let it multiply you. Brandish your suitcase like a plastic sword. Your legs switch calmly beneath you, a new power in them like antelopes, or turbines. Brush quickly past the ones who hold to the right, burdened by towers of luggage, placid and marveling. You are a marvel, a person with a plane to catch, whose arrival is awaited by others, whose stride grows longer and looser like a rodeo lasso thrown again and again over nothing, catching nothing but a ring of dust. The crowd going wildly opaque and at the end of it, a voice, brisk and comradely, giving you the old aching news.

THE MESSENGER (HER EARLY YEARS)

(K—5)

When I was small I loved the feel of a note safety-pinned to my chest, messages passed from mother to teacher and back again, loved to bear information on my body, the fluttering hands of women right there above my heart, pinning and unpinning their important and mysterious communiqués. Likewise, I loved the string pinned into my puffy winter coat that connected mitten to dangling mitten and traveled up one arm and down the other like a vein. Each year I was let out further and further on a longer and longer string, and I feared that at any second the string would jerk and reel me in like a hooked fish, or that one day the string would be cut and I would drift aimlessly from place to place, unknown by anyone and utterly free.

I'd rather tell about the snow, how overnight it turned our little alley into a sparkling tunnel, the snow whipped into huge drifts, which clung equally to the garbage cans and garage doors and the trees arched overhead. Then, how I tore a jagged line with my trudging legs in this perfect cylinder. When I got to school that day, my heart was beating very fast. I passed a note to my friend Roxanne which said, *I took some pills . . .*

(high school)

If you get this message, then beat a path to my door. If you appreciate my hairstyle, then tip the tornado. If you packed a suitcase, where would I hide in its satin folds? I ran away to Paris, and rolled in French dust under the Eiffel Tower, and bleached my hair the color of dingy snow, and ate 50 *centimes* burgers at McDonalds, and was kept by a series of brutal and romantic lovers, and I had no parents, and wore beautiful earrings and high leather boots, and discovered vodka, and was painted by all the great egoists, and never left home.

(college)

I fell in love with a woman who had many keys, a warden of sorts, and we led a purposeful and secluded life together. I inventoried my faults, and she helped me with that. In her room was a big picture window, from which I could see a tree on a far-away ridge, with branches that flared upward from its base in a shape like a flame. I was often naked in that cold room, but I would turn and turn and let the tree warm me. I wrote letters, comparing myself to the tree, and sent them to people I was certain no longer knew me.

DRY

When you're lost in the desert, it's important to collect your urine and any other liquid you produce to distill into drinking water using a tarp and two coffee cans. Most people, when getting lost, forget to bring the tarp and the coffee cans, so their urine is useless, their tears worse than useless, yet they continue to produce both and watch the tiny rivulets swallowed in seconds by parched and crackling dirt. For the desert, all your plump and watered hopes are just a drop on the tongue.

When the desert is lost in you, it sends out flags to other deserts. Hard crusts of dry skin form along your outer ridges. Your moisturizer fails. People start to steer clear of you, afraid you will "suck them dry." Only other desert people wander near, the ones who are further along than you. They wear their deserts on the outside. Wrapped head to toe like mummies in baroque tatters, moving their

sandpaper lips in crass imitation of language. *We know you,* they insist. *We're here for you.*

DREAM CATCHER

When calling after a receding dream, keep your eyes closed, let your mind go soft, and press your head just so into the pillow. It takes practice to walk between the worlds and so often the messages are dull and pedestrian, or else they are the un-nourished, malformed children we thought we'd left behind. How do they catch up to us on curled, boneless feet?

THE WORLD BELOW

The world's tallest trees are underwater where gravity can't get to them. They reach for a greenish blob of light, the mythical sun, which none have lived to see free of its wavering veil, for as soon as they puncture the surface, they are painfully burned on their uppermost new and tender leaves, and this kills them. It really does.

THE YUKON

The Yukon keeps me up at night, just knowing its vast coldness is up there, bleating in the dark. And landfills, who can forget landfills—the layers, the leachate, our lush, dark polyethylene hearts. And poor dethroned Pluto, emasculated god of the underworld, going around and around exactly like before. You can rest now, Sir. Nothing depends on you. You can lie awake beside me, let me whisper in your ear: *tundra, tundra.*

THE LAST BREAKUP

Well, I'm off! the soul chirps as it exits the body. From now on it will speak of the physical plane as "that old stomping ground" as if being yoked to flesh were a quaint nostalgia.

The body's hands dangle softly from its wrists like sapless leaves. There's so much room for improvement, even in death. Why couldn't it be wearing a silk pantsuit? Something coolly persuasive instead of this hot wool pathetic scratchy *you're leaving me* suit?

—And that tired hat collapsing in the sun of our burned-out love.

—That's no hat, that's my head!

—Exactly.

INSTRUCTIONS

If you can't reach it, leave it alone. Birds will pick it clean, or sharks or sunlight or the pincers of tiny carnivorous insects. If it's blown to bits in a public place or any place bits should not be, collect the bits and burn them. If it's just in a few pieces, make a small effort to reassemble the parts. I'm not talking major surgery (duh), just lay them close to where they were attached in life. If all parts are attached and body is gore-free, have a party! Wash me and comb my hair. Give me a manicure and a pedicure. Pluck the hairs from my chin and around my nipples. Put some nice white powder all over me, maybe some lavender and herbs. Do not let any creepy people participate, like _____ or _____. Wrap me in a sheet (organic cotton preferred, rain-washed and bleached in the sun) with just my face and hands showing for the viewing (and cute pedicured feet, but only if the room is very warm—I get so goddamned cold, you know). Make sure I look pretty! And invite every-

one who ever rejected me, especially _____.
Light the space with candles. Let people touch my
forehead with rosewater-moistened fingers. If they
are still alive, take a photograph of my mother and
father embracing for the first time since 1979. I
don't know why.

At the reception, sing songs. A good one is that
Freakwater song: "Heaven is for the weak at heart,
and those who never were as smart as me…"
What are some other ones? Cat Power has some
good ones, and the Carter Family. I'm sure Mom
knows some old Quaker death tunes to bring
down the house.

The next morning, bury me in the ground.

REMEMBER ME

If we should never meet again, remember I loved you as the sea loves the shore, loves to sob and rage against it, heaving up all sorts of dead and broken things.

IV

A WEDDING

They were wearing clothes they would never ordinarily wear.

The bride wore a lovely flowered sheath in muted tampon-applicator pink, and one of those half-sweaters which barely clasp the shoulders. Her nails were manicured, lavender.

The groom wore a charcoal suit and a pair of reading glasses on a cord around his neck, which stabbed at the chest of anyone who tried to hug him.

The bride's son wore a loud tie, though she was also a daughter. Also, s/he brought the music. Billie Holiday, but not the really sad stuff.

There had been some mistake about the food. An order from a different restaurant had been cancelled but was delivered anyway, to the wrong

address. Luckily, those people refused it.

The bride's niece was a kindergarten teacher, and told a horribly funny story at dinner: a student of hers had asked another teacher, who had very bad breath, *do you poop out of your mouth or your butt?*

The groom's brother had lately been suffering from dementia, and though there was no evidence of confusion on his part, he seemed anxious, as if fearful of spilling something on himself. He told the old story of how he'd lost his finger playing mumblypeg with a hatchet in the ravine, but with less gusto than he used to tell it.

There was enough lasagna to feed an army, but the chicken and potatoes went quickly.

The ceremony took place after dinner, to allow for everyone to cry more freely, being drunk.

The guests sat in a semi-circle around the couple, who were lit by a single *torchière*, a new word for most people. It refers, in this case, to a standing lamp with a shade like a calla lily, which throws its light up toward the ceiling.

The children stood and read quotations chosen from a book of quotations on the subject of marriage. The groom's son had to pronounce the words *My Lord*, and sounded very serious, almost angry, as he did so.

The groom's daughter hadn't gotten the e-mail asking everyone to prepare to offer a wish, and was silent during that portion of the ceremony.

Everyone was a little disappointed when the groom slipped the ring onto the bride's finger without saying in a fake Jersey accent, *No, wit dis ring, I thee wed.*

They forgot the marriage license and had to promise to drop it by in the morning.

In a digital photo of the event, printed that evening on a printer that was out of black ink, everybody's nostrils and the corners of their mouths appeared to be brimming with yellow-green bile. But this was not the case. Everyone was very happy.

FATHERS

Well-scrubbed schoolboys brandish their knitting needles for the war effort, as their trench-bound sisters pose for photos with their beaus, dole out promises of marriage upon sweet return, fill up on johnnycakes stacked high by nervous fathers, who tremble as they fuss with the lapels on their daughters' uniforms, stammering fatherly good-byes. Many a girl keeps a photograph of her father tucked in the jacket of a hard-bound book in her breast pocket. On at least one occasion that we know of, a bullet bound for the heart of a brave soldier tore through the pages of that book, stopping only at the last page, leaving her father's solemn face, and her heart, wholly intact.

194_
tear ducts stabbed to death by eyeliner pencil, film at eleven.

195_
push-up bra smothers woman in her own false hopes.

196_
wasp waist stings again!

197_
toxic smoke from bra-burnings poisons our nation's children, may be responsible for acid rain, decimation of the ozone layer, skyrocketing cancer rates.

198_

much sexual bruising caused by attempted splic-
ing of unpadded bodies, razor-sharp hip lacerates
unsuspecting tongue.

199_

couple linked for life in genital piercing circus act
gone awry.

200_

the world unbuttoned so quickly that we all died
from modesty.

MEN AND WOMEN

In the desert, men wander off after weather balloons, pants around their ankles. They'll fuck anything: vacuum cleaners, banana peels, the warm, creased liver of a just-slaughtered cow. And women. Ghostly women with red eyes. Women with nothing, who cannot feel their bodies, who are out for blood. Men will fuck them and suck on their numb breasts and think nothing of it. They suffer too, like little babies in incubators, tubes everywhere, who've never been held. It's nobody's fault.

TRIPLE EX

Last night he came to me with chapped and swollen lips. I had a balm on my fingertips, but I wouldn't touch him. Somewhere a wolf howled. Not touching him was the same as touching him.

OTHER

The other woman forfeits her right to be called a woman. She moves out of her apartment and into a cave, lives like a snarling thing, devoid of company, charmless. And still he comes to her, hurls his fresh carcass at her feet. His scent turns her back into a woman.

COVER

They cover each other, first with muck and straw and then with each other's flesh, thinking perhaps something will hatch out of this covering, this flap that rests over every thing. They wish to investigate all the ways in which a material can be said to lie atop another material, in layers, and what rests between the layers, whether sanctioned or soft or salted with grief.

Addendum
(glossary of terms)

(femme couverte)

The femme couverte is a gun for hire. Keep her in your century, a long-locked arsenal. She is not responsible for her actions. She owns nothing, not even herself. Women today are free, because we own things. Because we are held responsible.

A covered woman is warm, at least. Keep her in a covered wagon. All around it, arrows fly.

(finger)

1. The first time a boy fingered me I was too excited to move. After a while he asked me if I was dead.

2. To lay with blame. To remain blameless oneself. A finger jabbing at a photo, glossy and unreal, with real consequences for the jabbed. For the jabber also, though fewer studies have been done.

(fuck)

The quintessential Anglo-Saxon word, *fuck* starts soft and ends hard and, when said properly, leaves the mouth in perfect shape to receive penetration. Speaking the word is a form of foreplay, an incantation of things beyond our control. The front teeth brace themselves against the lower lip while the lungs force air between them. (To some the *f* sound conjures rabbits, stupid and weak-hearted. Others admire their softness and famed prolificacy.) Shifting into lower gear, the jaw goes slack and juts slightly forward, grazing hunger and privileging the bottom lip (sensuous) over the top lip (strict). Then comes a hard knock from the entrance to the throat like a brute hurling a bone against the wall of its cave.

For its mirror-sound, see *cuff*. A *fuck* spoken backwards can be a sharp blow or an instrument for encircling.

Too much emphasis has been placed on the f and the k. In fact, some people spell the word *f--k,* as Hebrews are compelled to write the word G-d, some things being too holy to be fully revealed. Vowels are rightly feared for their ability to shake the whole body if sustained for any length of time. Let us now give into the holy center of the *fuck,* the *uhhhhhhhhhhhhhhhh.* A groan, a rumbled sigh, an eternal plummeting.

(guilt)

A powerful aphrodisiac, long thought to be the especial province of adulterers and fundamentalists. Now it's been shown that no one is exempt. Even babies who touch themselves in their cribs have a nagging feeling they should be doing something more productive.

(hardtack a.k.a. "sailors' delight")

A lumpish food like a brick, gnawed on long voyages to stave off sexual violence. Two lumps rubbed together can, in a pinch, spark fire, yield a bit of warmth for the rather-go-hungry. Can be knotted in a sock and swung at enemy skulls or carved into a talisman for better luck next time. On land one could fashion an escape trowel.

Your sea choice is this: die fast or die slow, eat the prison or starve. Part bread part remorse, when added to the water of the body it reconstitutes into a murderous cloud. Red streaks in the tarry night. The body in mutiny—you never were its captain. Red-clotted morning and no one will come near you. Soon they'll just throw you over the side. Load your pockets with hardtack so you sink like a stone.

(hegemony)

Hegemony is one of those words that will make you sound smart, and allow you to extend your influence and dominate conversations on world affairs, but only if you pronounce it correctly. 82% of hot, smart girls in tight pants prefer a stress on the second syllable. Think gem, think Jiminy Cricket. Do not hedge, or moan.

(homeopathy)

When there is nothing left of me, I will become a remedy.

(Jiminy Cricket)

Jiminy Cricket is a slang term for Jesus Christ, for those whose superstitions prevent them from taking the "Lord's name" in vain when they encounter pain, shock, orgasm,* disbelief. J.C. played the comic foil and supposed conscience of a certain long-nosed liar, and also appeared in numerous safety films, warning children of the dangers of household poisons, old refrigerators, and live wires. In the original book version of Pinocchio, he was smashed (crucified?) early in the story, but continued on as a ghostly adviser.

Just imagine the god-fearing in their stark beds, whether in strange dreams or the neverland of non-procreative sex, encountering mystery without the benefit of strong expletives. Such nakedness we whores will never know.

Sarah Fran Wisby grew up in Evanston, Illinois, attended Goddard College in Plainfield, Vermont, and received her MFA in creative writing from San Francisco State University. She lives, works, and writes in the Mission District of San Francisco.